Plan

Every Day is Malala Day

Rosemary McCarney with Plan International

New Internationalist

Who is Malala?

On October 9, 2012, a fifteen-year-old girl on her way to school in Pakistan was shot in the head by a member of the Taliban. Malala Yousafzai had been speaking out in public about the right of all girls to have an education – something the Taliban were against. They thought that shooting her would stop her campaign, but they didn't know how strong Malala is. She was flown to England for life-saving treatment, and has recovered. Malala and two other girls who were wounded in the attack are attending school and living in England. Malala is more determined than ever to work for every child's right to an education. For her bravery and effort on behalf of all children, she has received almost thirty awards and honors, including Pakistan's National Youth Peace Prize, the KidsRights International Children's Peace Prize, President Clinton's Global Citizen Award, the Ambassador of Conscience Award from Amnesty International, and the Freedom of Thought Prize from the European Parliament. In 2013, Malala Yousafzai became the youngest person ever nominated for the Nobel Peace Prize.

Peru

Dear Malala,

Niger

We have never met before, but I feel like I know you.

El Salvador

I have never seen you before, but I've heard your voice.

Indonesia

To girls like me, you are a leader who encourages us.
And you are a friend.

...discrimination...

Indonesia

...violence...all play a part.

Kenya

But because you are a girl, you have shown
the world that these things will not stop you.

You, Malala, have reminded us that it is your right
– my right – *every* child's right to go to school.

India

Instead of living in fear…

Kenya

...we must shout for change.

Because I am a girl, I am writing to
let you know that every day is Malala Day.

Girls everywhere are behind you.

Nepal

Uganda

We are raising our hands with you…

Germany

Niger

...as you represent all of us.

United States

The world will see what girls can achieve – if only they let us.

On July 12, 2013, the day of her 16th birthday, Malala Yousafzai stood to speak to nearly 1,000 delegates to the United Nations' Youth Assembly. The Secretary General of the UN had just proclaimed that day to be Malala Day. Here are parts of Malala Yousafzai's speech.

"So here I stand…one girl among many. I speak – not for myself, but for all girls and boys. I raise up my voice – not so that I can shout, but so that those without a voice can be heard. Those who have fought for their rights: their right to live in peace; their right to be treated with dignity; their right to equality of opportunity; their right to be educated.

Dear Friends, on the 9th of October 2012, the Taliban shot me on the left side of my forehead. They shot my friends, too. They thought that the bullets would silence us.

But they failed. Weakness, fear, and hopelessness died. Strength, power, and courage were born. I am the same Malala. My ambitions are the same. My hopes are the same. My dreams are the same.

We want schools and education for every child's bright future. We will continue our journey to our destination of peace and education for everyone. No one can stop us. We will speak for our rights and we will bring change through our voice. We must believe in the power and the strength of our words. Our words can change the world. Because we are all together, united for the cause of education. And if we want to achieve our goal, then let us empower ourselves with the weapon of knowledge and let us shield ourselves with unity and togetherness.

Dear brothers and sisters, we must not forget that millions of people are suffering from poverty, injustice, and ignorance. We must not forget that millions of children are out of schools. We must not forget that our sisters and brothers are waiting for a bright peaceful future.

So let us wage a global struggle against illiteracy, poverty, and terrorism and let us pick up our books and pens. They are our most powerful weapons.

One child, one teacher, one pen, and one book can change the world.

Education is the only solution. Education First."

Photo Credits

Acknowledgments

Many hands created this beautiful tribute to a remarkable young woman. The Plan International Communications team was inspired by the United Nations declaring July 12, 2013 Malala Day, when 500 young people "took over" the UN for the first time with the ready support of the UN Secretary General. They produced a short film depicting girls from all over the world writing to Malala to tell her how important a symbol she was for them in their lives. Jen Albaugh took this warm and powerful video and helped me turn it into this book, choosing the incredible photographs Plan has collected from all over the world to bring the girls' words to life. Malala's charm, courage, and conviction are an inspiration to all of them and to all of us. Heartfelt thanks to all of the Plan teams who helped me bring this story to life.

—*Rosemary McCarney*

Every Day is Malala Day
Published in 2016
New Internationalist Publications Ltd
The Old Music Hall
106-108 Cowley Road
Oxford OX4 1JE, UK
newint.org

Published by permission of Second Story Press, Toronto,
Ontario, Canada.

Printed and bound in China.

British Library Cataloguing-in-Publication Data.
A catalogue record for this book is available from the
British Library.

ISBN 978-1-78026-326-7

This book is dedicated to
the other 65 million girls in
the world today who are
neither in primary school nor
secondary school.